Wool of the Andes

2013 COLLECTION

by Knit Picks

Printed in the United States of America

First Printing, 2013

ISBN 978-1-67267-006-7

Versa Press, Inc
800-447-7829

www.versapress.com

CONTENTS

Retro Cabled Cardigan   6

Insulate   12

Bayr Pullover   18

Arrows Hat & Mitts   24

Ambers Pullover & Hat   28

Reilly Afghan   34

RETRO CABLED CARDIGAN

by Vanessa Ewing

FINISHED MEASUREMENTS

34, (38, 42, 46, 50, 54)" finished bust measurement buttoned; garment is meant to be worn with approximately 2-4" of positive ease.

22, (23, 24, 25, 26, 27)" long

18.5, (18.5, 19, 19, 19. 19)" sleeve length, from underarm

YARN

Knit Picks Wool of the Andes Tweed (80% Peruvian Highland Wool, 20 % Donegal Tweed; 110 yards/50g): Brass Heather 25451, 11, (13, 15, 17, 18, 20) balls.

NEEDLES

US 8 (5mm) 24" or longer circular needles, or size to obtain gauge

NOTIONS

Yarn Needle
Stitch Markers
Scrap yarn or stitch holder
7 buttons

GAUGE

18 sts and 26 rows = 4" over stockinette stitch, blocked (see blocking instructions under Finishing)

20 sts and 26 rows = 4" over cable pattern, blocked (see blocking instructions under Finishing)

Retro Cabled Cardigan

Notes:

This unisex cabled cardigan features a simple cable pattern that is made without a cable needle. The retro cardigan has about 2-4" of positive ease, and features patch pockets and elbows. 60's influence with an urban vibe!

Cable Stitch Pattern (multiple of 4 sts + 2)

Row 1 (WS): K2, *P2, K2; rep from * across.

Row 2: P2, *K into the front of the second stitch on the left hand needle- do not slip off, K into the front of the first stitch, slip both off the needle, P2; rep from * across.

Elbow Patch Cable (EPC- worked over 2 sts)

K into the front of the second stitch on the left hand needle - do not slip off, K into the front of the first stitch, slip both sts off the needle.

Stockinette Stitch (St st)

Knit on the right side of work and purl on the wrong side of work.

DIRECTIONS

Back

Cast on 86, (98, 106, 118, 126, 138) sts. Work in Cable Stitch Pattern for 10 rows, starting with row 1.

Decrease Row (WS): Purl across row, decreasing 8, (10, 10, 12, 12, 14) sts evenly across.

78, (88, 96, 106, 114, 124) sts. Begin working in st st, starting with a knit row. When back measures 13.5", (14, 14.5, 15, 15.5, 16) from cast on edge, end having worked a WS Row.

Increase Row (RS): Knit across row, increasing 8, (10, 10, 12, 12, 14) sts evenly across.

86, (98, 106, 118, 126, 138) sts.

Begin working in Cable Stitch Pattern, starting with row 1.

When back measures 14.5", (15, 15.5, 16, 16.5, 17) from cast on edge, end having worked a WS Row.

Shape Armholes: Bind off 5, (6, 7, 8, 9, 10) sts at the beginning of next 2 rows.

76, (86, 92, 102, 108, 118) sts.

Bind off 0, (0, 0, 2, 3, 4) sts at the beginning of next 2 rows. 76, (86, 92, 98, 102, 110) sts.

Decrease Row (RS): K2, ssk, work in Cable Stitch Pattern to last 4 sts, k2tog, k2.

Next Row (WS): P3, work in Cable Stitch Pattern to last 3 sts, p3.

Repeat the last 2 rows 6, (8, 9, 9, 9, 10) times more. 62, (68, 72, 78, 82, 88) sts.

Keeping the first and last 3 sts in st st, continue to work in established Cable Stitch Pattern until armhole measures 7", (7.5, 8, 8.5, 9, 9.5).

Shape Shoulders: Bind off 8, (8, 9, 10, 11, 12) sts at the beginning

of next 2 rows.

Bind off 7, (8, 9, 10, 11, 12) at the beginning of next 2 rows.

Place remaining 32, (36, 36, 38, 38, 40) sts onto a stitch holder or scrap yarn.

Right Front

Cast on 42, (46, 50, 54, 58, 66) sts.

Work in Cable Stitch Pattern for 10 rows, starting with row 1.

Decrease Row (WS): Purl across all sts, decreasing 5, (4, 4, 3, 3, 6) sts evenly across.

37, (42, 46, 51, 55, 60) sts.

Begin working in st st, starting with a knit row.

When front measures 13.5", (14, 14.5, 15, 15.5, 16) from cast on edge, end having worked a WS Row.

Increase Row (RS): Knit across all sts, increasing 5, (4, 4, 3, 3, 6) sts evenly across.

42, (46, 50, 54, 58, 66) sts.

Begin working in Cable Stitch Pattern, starting with row 1.

When front measures 14.5", (15, 15.5, 16, 16.5, 17) from cast on edge, end having worked a RS Row.

Shape Armholes (WS): Bind off 5, (6, 7, 8, 9, 10) sts, work in established Cable Stitch Patternto end of row. 37, (40, 43, 46, 49, 56) sts. Work in established Cable Stitch Patternto end of row. Bind off 0, (0, 0, 2, 3, 4) sts, work in established Cable Stitch Patternto end of row. 37, (40, 43, 44, 46, 52) sts.

Decrease Row (RS): Work in established Cable Stitch Patternto last 4 sts, k2tog, k2.

Next Row (WS): P3, work in established Cable Stitch Patternto end of row.

Repeat the last 2 rows 6, (8, 9, 9, 9, 10) times more. 30, (31, 33, 34, 36, 41) sts.

Keeping the last 3 sts in st st, continue to work in established Cable Stitch Patternuntil front measures 19" (20, 21, 22, 23, 24) from cast on edge, end having worked a WS Row.

Shape Neck (RS): K7, (7, 7, 7, 7, 9) and place these 7, (7, 7, 7, 7, 9) sts onto a holder, work in established Cable Stitch Patternto end of row.

23, (24, 26, 27, 29, 32) sts.

Next Row (WS): P3 work in established Cable Stitch Patternto last 3 sts, p3.

Next Row (RS): K2 ssk, work in established Cable Stitch Patternto last 3 sts, k3.

Repeat the last 2 rows 7, (7, 7, 6, 6, 7) times more. 15, (16, 18, 20, 22, 24) sts.

Continue to work even on remaining sts, keeping the first and last 3 sts of every row in st st. At the same time when armhole measures 7", (7.5, 8, 8.5, 9, 9.5), end having worked a RS Row.

Shape Shoulder (WS): Bind off 8, (8, 9, 10, 11, 12) sts, work in established Cable Stitch Patternto last 3 sts, p3.

Next Row (RS): K3, work in established Cable Stitch Patternto end of row.

Bind off remaining 7, (8, 9, 10, 11, 12) sts.

Left Front

Work same as right front, reversing all shaping.

Sleeves (Make 2 the same)

The sleeves are worked flat from the wrists/cuff up to the cap.

Cast on 42, (42, 46, 46, 50, 50) sts. Work in Cable Stitch Patternfor 10 rows, starting with row 1.

Decrease Row (WS): Purl across row, decreasing 4 sts evenly across.

38, (38, 42, 42, 46, 46) sts. Begin working in st st, starting with a knit row.

Increase 1 st at each end of every10th, (8th, 8th, 7th, 7th, 6th) row 9, (11, 12, 14, 14, 16)times. 56, (60, 66, 70, 74, 78) sts.

Work even until sleeve measures 17.5", (17.5, 18, 18, 18, 18) from cast on edge, end having worked a WS Row.

Increase Row (RS): Knit across row, increasing 6, (6, 8, 8, 8, 8) sts evenly across.

62, (66, 74, 78, 82, 86) sts. Begin working inCable Stitch Pattern, starting with row 1.

When sleeve measures 18.5", (18.5, 19, 19, 19, 19) from cast on edge, end having worked a WS Row.

Shape Armholes: Bind off 5, (6, 7, 8, 9, 10) sts at the beginning of next 2 rows.

52, (54, 60, 62, 64, 66) sts.

Bind off 0, (0, 0, 2, 3, 4) sts at the beginning of next 2 rows. 52, (54, 60, 58, 58, 58) sts.

Decrease Row (RS): K2 ssk, work in Cable Stitch Patternto last 4 sts, k2tog, k2.

Next Row (WS): P3, work in Cable Stitch Patternto last 3 sts, p3.

Repeat the last 2 rows 14, (14, 14, 13, 13, 13) times more. 22, (24, 30, 30, 30, 30) sts.Then bind off 3, (2, 3, 2, 2, 2) sts at the beginning of next 4 rows. Bind off remaining 10, (16, 18, 22, 22, 22) sts.

Pockets (make 2)

Cast on 25 sts. Work in st st for 5.5", end having worked a WS Row- increasing 1 st across last row. 26 sts. Work in Cable Stitch Patternfor 1". Bind off all sts on next RS Row.

Elbow Patches (make 2)

Cast on 8 sts.

Row 1 (WS): P1, k2, *p2, k2; rep from * to last st, p1.
Row 2: K1, m1, p2, EPC, P2, m1, k1. 10 sts.
Row 3: *P2, k2; rep from * across, p2.
Row 4: K1, m1, k1, p2, EPC, P2, k1, m1, k1. 12 sts.
Row 5: P3, k2, p2, k2, p3.
Row 6: K1, m1, (EPC, p2)2x, EPC, m1, k1. 14 sts.
Row 7: P1, k1, (p2, k2)2x, p2, k1, p1.
Row 8: K1, m1, p1, (EPC, p2)2x, EPC, p1, m1, k1. 16 sts.
Row 9: P1, k2, (p2, k2)3x, p1.
Row 10: K1, p2, (EPC, P2)3x, k1.
Row 11: P1, k2, (p2, k2)3x, p1.
Rows 12-21: Repeatrows 10 and 11.
Row 22: Ssk, p1, (EPC, p2)2x,EPC, P1, k2tog. 14 sts.
Row 23: P1, k1, (p2, k2)2x, p2, k1, p1.
Row 24: Ssk, (EPC, P2)2x, EPC, k2tog. 12 sts.
Row 25: P3, (k2, p2)2x, p1.
Row 26: Ssk, k1, p2, EPC, P2, k1, k2tog. 10 sts.
Row 27: P2, (k2, p2)2x.
Row 28: Ssk, p2, EPC, P2, k2tog. 8 sts.
Row 29: P1, k2, p2, k2, p1.
Row 30: Ssk, p1, EPC, P1, k2tog. 6 sts.

Bind off all sts in pattern. Cut yarn and leave a long tail for sewing.

Finishing

Soak the garment in your favorite wool wash, do not over agitate. Roll in towels to remove most of the moisture. Shape to finished garment measurements and let air dry. Be aware the schematic measurements do not include selvedge sts, when blocking before seaming add 0.4" in width to the Back, Fronts, and Sleeves.Sew shoulder seams. Easesleeves into armholes and sew in place. Sew side and sleeve seams.

Buttonhole band: With RS facing, working from bottom edge, pick up and knit 94, (98, 106, 110, 118, 122) sts along the right front.

Work 4 rows ofCable Stitch Patternstarting with row 1.

Buttonhole Row (WS): Work pattern for 10 sts, *bind off 2 sts, pattern 14, (15, 17, 17, 19, 20) sts; rep from * 4 times more, bind off 2 sts, pattern to end of row.

Next Row: Work across all sts in pattern stitch, casting on 2 sts over each bound off section. Work 3 more rows in Cable Stitch Patternand bind off all sts in pattern on next row.

Buttonband: With RS facingand working from top edge, pick up and knit 94, (98, 106, 110, 118, 122) sts along the left front. Work 9 rows of Cable Stitch Pattern, starting with row 1. Bind off all sts on next row in pattern.

Neckband: With RS facing, pick up and knit 8 sts on top of the right front buttonhole band, k7, (7, 7, 7, 7, 9)heldsts from right front neck, pick up and knit 16 sts from neck edge to shoulder, k32, (36, 36, 38, 38, 40) from back holder- increasing 0, (0, 0, 2, 2, 4) sts evenly across, pick up and knit 16 sts from left front neck edge to holder, k7, (7, 7, 7, 7, 9) sts from holder, pick up 8 sts along the buttonband. 94 (98, 98, 102, 102, 110) sts.

Work inCable Stitch Pattern, starting with row 1.

Next Row (RS): Pattern 4 sts, bind off 2 sts, pattern to end of row.

On next row, pattern to bind off sts, cast on 2 sts over bound off section, pattern to end.

Work until neckband measures 1 ¼" from pick up row. Bind off all sts in pattern on next RS Row.

Sew pockets onto left and right front, just above the ribbing. Whipstitch the sides of the elbow patches down to the sleeves. Weave in ends, wash and block to diagram. Sew on 7 buttons onto the left front buttonband.

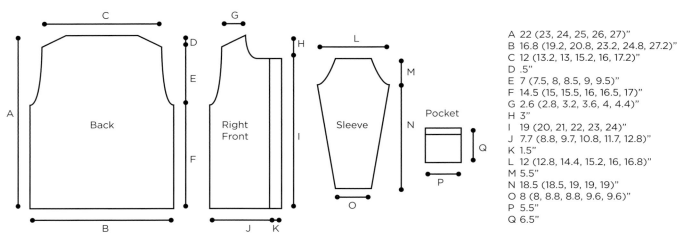

A 22 (23, 24, 25, 26, 27)"
B 16.8 (19.2, 20.8, 23.2, 24.8, 27.2)"
C 12 (13.2, 13, 15.2, 16, 17.2)"
D .5"
E 7 (7.5, 8, 8.5, 9, 9.5)"
F 14.5 (15, 15.5, 16, 16.5, 17)"
G 2.6 (2.8, 3.2, 3.6, 4, 4.4)"
H 3"
I 19 (20, 21, 22, 23, 24)"
J 7.7 (8.8, 9.7, 10.8, 11.7, 12.8)"
K 1.5"
L 12 (12.8, 14.4, 15.2, 16, 16.8)"
M 5.5"
N 18.5 (18.5, 19, 19, 19)"
O 8 (8, 8.8, 8.8, 9.6, 9.6)"
P 5.5"
Q 6.5"

Measurements do not include selvedge sts, when blocking before seaming add 0.4" in width to the Back, Fronts, and Sleeves.

Abbreviations							
BO	bind off	K-wise	knitwise	PU	pick up	SSP	sl, sl, p these 2 sts tog tbl
cn	cable needle	LH	left hand	P-wise	purlwise		
CC	contrast color	M	marker	rep	repeat	SSSK	sl, sl, sl, k these 3 sts tog
CDD	Centered double dec	M1	make one stitch	Rev St st	reverse stockinette stitch	St st	stockinette stitch
CO	cast on	M1L	make one left-leaning stitch	RH	right hand	sts	stitch(es)
cont	continue	M1R	make one right-leaning stitch	rnd(s)	round(s)	TBL	through back loop
dec	decrease(es)			RS	right side	TFL	through front loop
DPN(s)	double pointed needle(s)	MC	main color	Sk	skip	tog	together
		P	purl	Sk2p	sl 1, k2tog, pass slipped stitch over k2tog: 2 sts dec	W&T	wrap & turn (see specific instructions in pattern)
EOR	every other row	P2tog	purl 2 sts together				
inc	increase	PM	place marker	SKP	sl, k, psso: 1 st dec	WE	work even
K	knit	PFB	purl into the front and back of stitch	SL	slip	WS	wrong side
K2tog	knit two sts together			SM	slip marker	WYIB	with yarn in back
		PSSO	pass slipped stitch over	SSK	sl, sl, k these 2 sts tog	WYIF	with yarn in front
KFB	knit into the front					YO	yarn over

INSULATE

by Christina Harris

FINISHED MEASUREMENTS

32 (34, 36, 38, 40, 42, 44)(46, 48, 50, 52, 54)" finished bust measurement; garment is meant to be worn with 2-3" of positive ease.

YARN

Knit Picks Wool of the Andes Worsted (100% Peruvian Highland Wool; 110 yards/50g), Currant 24647: 12 (12, 13, 13, 14, 15, 16)(17, 17, 18, 19, 19) balls

NEEDLES

US 7 (4.5mm) DPNs, 16" and 32" circular needles, or size to obtain gauge
US 6 (4mm) DPNs, 16" and 32" circular needles, or one size smaller than that used to obtain gauge

NOTIONS

Removable and circular stitch markers
Cable needle
Scrap yarn or stitch holders
7-9 buttons 1.25" diameter

GAUGE

20 sts and 26 rows = 4" over stockinette on larger needles, and 22 sts over Chart B, blocked.

Insulate

Notes:

The sweater is worked from the top down, back and forth, in one piece. Short rows shape the shoulders as well as the tops of the sleeves. Cables are continuously worked on both body and sleeves.

You may wish to underline stitch counts specific to your size throughout the pattern for clarity.

Seed Stitch Pattern (worked flat)
Row 1: (K1, P1) to end.
Row 2: (P1, K1) to end.

Pattern is worked over both odd and even numbers of sts throughout the pattern. K sts on the first row will be knit into on the second, and P sts on the first row will be purled into on the second.

Seed Stitch Pattern (in the round)
Round 1: (K1, P1) to end.
Round 2: (P1, K1) to end.

Pattern is worked over both odd and even numbers of sts on the sleeves. K sts on the first round will be purled into on the second, and P sts on the first round will be knit into on the second.

Backwards loop cast on
Loop working yarn and place it on needle backward so it doesn't unwind. Repeat for as many stitches as you need.

Cable cast on (for buttonholes)
Insert the needle between the first two stitches in the left hand needle, wrap and bring through. Transfer the newly created stitch onto the left hand needle. Repeat for as many stitches as you need.

DIRECTIONS
Collar
With 16" smaller circ needles, CO 100 (102, 102, 102, 102, 104, 110) (116, 118, 120, 122, 124) sts.

Row 1 (WS): *K1, p1 (seed st) for 10 (10, 10, 10, 10, 10, 12)(12, 12, 12, 13, 13) sts, pm. Seed st (cont from prev pattern) for 5 (5, 5, 5, 5, 5, 5)(6, 6, 6, 6, 6) sts, p3, seed st for 7 sts, p3, seed st for 5 (5, 5, 5, 5, 5, 5)(6, 6, 6, 6, 6) sts, pm. Seed st for 34 (36, 36, 36, 36, 38, 40)(42, 44, 46, 46, 48) sts, pm, seed st 5 (5, 5, 5, 5, 5, 5)(6, 6, 6, 6, 6) sts, p3, seed st for 7 sts, p3, seed st for 5 (5, 5, 5, 5, 5, 5)(6, 6, 6, 6, 6), pm, seed st for 10 (10, 10, 10, 10, 10, 12)(12, 12, 12, 13, 13) sts.

Row 2 (RS): Seed st for 10 (10, 10, 10, 10, 10, 12)(12, 12, 12, 13, 13) sts, sm, seed st for 5 (5, 5, 5, 5, 5, 5)(6, 6, 6, 6, 6) sts, k3, seed st for 7 sts, k3, seed st for 5 (5, 5, 5, 5, 5, 5)(6, 6, 6, 6, 6) sts, sm, seed st for 34 (36, 36, 36, 36, 38, 40)(42, 44, 46, 46, 48) sts, sm, seed st for 5 (5, 5, 5, 5, 5, 5)(6, 6, 6, 6, 6) sts, k3, seed st for 7 sts, k3, seed st for 5 (5, 5, 5, 5, 5, 5)(6, 6, 6, 6, 6) sts, sm, seed st for 10 (10, 10, 10, 10, 10, 12)(12, 12, 12, 13, 13) sts.

Repeat Rows 1 and 2 for a total of 14 rows.

Row 15 (WS) Chart Set Up: Change to larger size 16" circ needles. K2, p4, k 4 (4, 4, 4, 4, 4, 6)(6, 6, 6, 7, 7), sm, k 5 (5, 5, 5, 5, 5, 5)(6, 6, 6, 6, 6), p13, k 5 (5, 5, 5, 5, 5, 5)(6, 6, 6, 6, 6), sm, k 4 (4, 4, 4, 4, 4, 6)(6, 6, 6, 7, 7), p4, k 18 (20, 20, 20, 20, 22, 24)(26, 28, 30, 30, 32), p4, k4, sm, k 4 (4, 4, 4, 4, 4, 6)(6, 6, 6, 7, 7), p13, k 5 (5, 5, 5, 5, 5, 5)(6, 6, 6, 6, 6), sm, k 4 (4, 4, 4, 4, 4, 6)(6, 6, 6, 7, 7), p4, k2.

Row 16 (RS): P2, work row 1 of Chart A, p 4 (4, 4, 4, 4, 4, 6)(6, 6, 6, 7, 7), sm, p 5 (5, 5, 5, 5, 5, 5)(6, 6, 6, 6, 6), work row 1 of Chart B, p 5 (5, 5, 5, 5, 5, 5)(6, 6, 6, 6, 6), sm (these sts just knit between markers are the shoulder saddle sts), p4, work row 1 of Chart A, p 18 (20, 20, 20, 20, 22, 24)(26, 28, 30, 30, 32), work row 1 of Chart A, p4, sm, p 5 (5, 5, 5, 5, 5, 5)(6, 6, 6, 6, 6), work row 1 of Chart B, p 5 (5, 5, 5, 5, 5, 5)(6, 6, 6, 6, 6), sm, p 4 (4, 4, 4, 4, 4, 6)(6, 6, 6, 7, 7), work row 1 of Chart A, p2.

Row 17 (WS): K2, work row 2 of Chart A, k 4 (4, 4, 4, 4, 4, 6)(6, 6, 6, 7, 7), sm, k 5 (5, 5, 5, 5, 5, 5)(6, 6, 6, 6, 6), work row 2 of Chart B, k 5 (5, 5, 5, 5, 5, 5)(6, 6, 6, 6, 6), sm, k4, work row 2 of Chart A, k 18 (20, 20, 20, 20, 22, 24)(26, 28, 30, 30, 32), work row 2 of Chart A, k4, sm, k 5 (5, 5, 5, 5, 5, 5)(6, 6, 6, 6, 6), work row 2 of Chart B, k 5 (5, 5, 5, 5, 5, 5)(6, 6, 6, 6, 6), sm, k 4 (4, 4, 4, 4, 4, 6)(6, 6, 6, 7, 7), work row 2 of Chart A, k2.

Repeat rows 16 and 17 (continuing through Chart B) for 5" from cast on edge, or desired height of collar, ending with a WS row and noting which line of Chart B you just completed.

Next row: Break yarn and place left front sts (between end and marker) on a holder. Place left shoulder saddle sts (sts between markers) on 16" larger circ needles or dpns, join yarn and continue on these 23 (23, 23, 23, 23, 23, 23)(25, 25, 25, 25, 25) sts only, working Chart B as est. and knitting the first st of every row to make picking sts up later easier. Work until piece measures 3 (3.5, 3.5, 3.75, 4, 4.5, 4.75)(5, 5, 5, 5.25)", ending with a RS row and noting which row of the chart you ended on. Break yarn and place sts on holder.

Place right front sts (between other end and marker) on a holder. Place right shoulder sts on dpns, join yarn and work as per left side. Break yarn and place sts on holder.

Back
Using larger size 32" circ needles and with RS facing and beginning at last left shoulder saddle row worked, pick up and purl 4 (5, 5, 6, 6, 7, 8)(9, 9, 9, 9, 10) sts along edge, then pick up and knit 8 sts, then pick up and purl 4 (5, 5, 6, 6, 7, 8)(9, 9, 9, 9, 10) sts. 16 (18, 18, 20, 20, 22, 24)(26, 26, 26, 26, 28) sts total, ending at neck edge. Pm.

On back of neck sts, p4, work row 1 of Chart A, p 18 (20, 20, 20, 20, 22, 24)(26, 28, 30, 30, 32), work row 1 of Chart A, p4.

Pm, then on right saddle pick up and purl 4 (5, 5, 6, 6, 7, 8)(9, 9, 9, 9, 10) sts, pick up and knit 8 sts, then pick up and purl 4 (5, 5, 6, 6, 7, 8)(9, 9, 9, 9, 10) sts.

66 (72, 72, 76, 76, 82, 88)(94, 96, 98, 98, 104) sts total.

Next row (WS): K 4 (5, 5, 6, 6, 7, 8)(9, 9, 9, 9, 10), p2, (M1P, p1) 5 times, p1, k 4 (5, 5, 6, 6, 7, 8)(9, 9, 9, 9, 10). 5 sts incr'd. Sm, work across back sts working Chart A sts as you come to them, sm. K 4 (5, 5, 6, 6, 7, 8)(9, 9, 9, 9, 10), p2, (M1P, p1) 5 times, p1, k 4 (5, 5, 6, 6, 7, 8)(9, 9, 9, 9, 10). 5 sts incr'd.

76 (82, 82, 86, 86, 92, 98)(104, 106, 108, 108, 114) sts total.

Shape shoulders

Continue to work row 1 of Chart A on RS rows and row 2 on WS rows, while working short rows to shape shoulders as follows:

Next row (RS): P 4 (5, 5, 6, 6, 7, 8)(9, 9, 9, 9, 10), k13, p 4 (5, 5, 6, 6, 7, 8)(9, 9, 9, 9, 10), sm, work across back sts, sm. P 4 (5, 5, 6, 6, 7, 8)(9, 9, 9, 9, 10) sts. Wrap the next st as follows: Move yarn to opposite side of the work between needles, slip next st to right-hand needle, bring yarn around this st to original side of work, slip st back to left-hand needle, then turn work to begin working back in the other direction.

Next row (WS): Work to the second marker, then work 4 (5, 5, 6, 6, 7, 8)(9, 9, 9, 9, 10) sts, wrap the next st and turn.

Working the wraps tog with the sts as you come to them, work to 4 (5, 5, 5, 6, 7, 7)(7, 7, 7, 8, 8) sts past the last turning point on the next two rows.

Wrap the next st and turn the work. Then work 5 (6, 6, 6, 7, 7, 8)(8, 8, 8, 8, 9) sts past the last turning point on the next two rows.

Next row (RS): Work to end, removing markers as you go, and starting line 1 of Chart B on each set of 13 knit sts.

Work back and forth in rows across all sts, working Charts A and B until piece measures 6 (6.25, 6.25, 6.25, 6.25, 6.5, 6.75)(6.5, 6.75, 6.5, 6.25, 6.5)" from the shoulder line in the center of the saddle, along armhole edge, and ending with a WS row. Note which line of Chart B you are on.

Shape armholes

Increase 1 st at each armhole edge every RS row 3 (2, 3, 4, 5, 5, 5)(6, 6, 8, 9, 9) times.

Then CO 3 sts at the beg of each armhole edge, ending with a WS row. 88 (92, 94, 100, 102, 108, 114)(122, 124, 130, 132, 138) sts total.

Piece measures approx. 7.5 (7.5, 7.5, 7.75, 8, 8.25, 8.5)(8.5, 8.75, 9, 9.25, 9.5)". Leave sts on needles and cut yarn.

Left Front

Using larger size 16" circ needles or dpns, and with RS facing and beg at left front edge, p2, work row 1 of Chart A, p 4 (4, 4, 4, 4, 4, 6)(6, 6, 6, 7, 7). Then pick up and purl 4 (5, 5, 6, 6, 7, 8)(9, 9, 9, 9, 10) sts, pick up and knit 8 sts, then pick up and purl 4 (5, 5, 6, 6, 7, 8)(9, 9, 9, 9, 10) sts along left saddle. 26 (28, 28, 30, 30, 32, 36)(38, 38, 38, 39, 41) sts total.

Next row (WS): K 4 (5, 5, 6, 6, 7, 8)(9, 9, 9, 9, 10), p2, (M1P, p1) 5 times, p1, k 8 (9, 9, 10, 10, 11, 14)(15, 15, 15, 16, 17), work row 2 of Chart A, k2. 5 sts incr'd. 31 (33, 33, 35, 35, 37, 41)(43, 43, 43, 44, 46) sts total.

Next row (RS): P2, work row 1 of Chart A, p 8 (9, 9, 10, 10, 11, 14)(15, 15, 15, 16, 17), start on row 31 of Chart B over next 13 sts, p 4 (5, 5, 6, 6, 7, 8)(9, 9, 9, 9, 10). Continue, working Charts A and B, until piece measures the same length as back, and is on same line of Chart B as back, to beg of armhole shaping, measured along armhole edge, ending with a WS row.

Shape Armhole

Inc 1 st at armhole edge every 2nd row (RS row) 3 (2, 3, 4, 5, 5, 5)(5, 6, 8, 9, 9) times. Then CO 3 sts at armhole edge once. Work 1 WS row.

Front has 37 (38, 39, 42, 43, 45, 49,)(51, 52, 54, 56, 58) sts and measures same as back.

Right Front

Using larger size 16" circ needles or dpns, and with RS facing and beg at end of saddle, pick up and purl 4 (5, 5, 6, 6, 7, 8)(9, 9, 9, 9, 10) sts, pick up and knit 8 sts, then pick up and purl 4 (5, 5, 6, 6, 7, 8)(9, 9, 9, 9, 10) sts, along right saddle, ending at neck edge. Then p 4 (4, 4, 4, 4, 4, 6)(6, 6, 6, 7, 7), work row 1 of Chart A, p2. 26 (28, 28, 30, 30, 32, 36)(38, 38, 38, 39, 41) sts total.

Next row (WS): K2, work row 2 of Chart A, k 8 (9, 9, 10, 10, 11, 14)(15, 15, 15, 16, 17), p2, (M1P, p1) 5 times, p1, k 4 (5, 5, 6, 6, 7, 8)(9, 9, 9, 10). 5 sts incr'd. 31 (33, 33, 35, 35, 37, 41)(43, 43, 43, 44, 46) sts total.

Next row (RS): P 4 (5, 5, 6, 6, 7, 8)(9, 9, 9, 9, 10) start on row 31 of Chart B over next 13 sts, p 8 (9, 9, 10, 10, 11, 14)(15, 15, 15, 16, 17), row 1 of Chart A, p2. Continue, working Charts A and B, until piece measures the same length as back, and is on same line of Chart B as back, to beg of armhole shaping, measured along armhole edge, ending with a WS row.

Shape Armhole

Inc 1 st at armhole edge every 2nd row (RS row) 3 (2, 3, 4, 5, 5, 5)(5, 6, 8, 9, 9) times. Then CO 3 sts at armhole edge once. Work 1 WS row.

Front has 37 (38, 39, 42, 43, 45, 49)(51, 52, 54, 56, 58) sts and measures same as back.

Lower Body

Continue working Charts A and B down the body until reaching the seed st hem.

Joining row: With RS facing, and using left side of larger size 32" circ needle holding back sts, work 37 (38, 39, 42, 43, 45, 49)(51, 52, 54, 56, 58) sts of left front, pm, then using backwards loop method CO 8 (8, 10, 10, 10, 10, 10)(10, 12, 12, 12, 14) sts, pm. Work 88 (92, 94, 100, 102, 108, 114)(122, 124, 130, 132, 138) sts on back, pm and CO 8 (8, 10, 10, 10, 10, 10, 12)(12, 12, 14) sts, pm. Then work 37 (38, 39, 42, 43, 45, 49)(51, 52, 54, 56, 58) sts on right front. 178 (184, 192, 204, 208, 218, 232)(244, 252, 262, 268, 282) sts total.

Next row (WS): Work to first marker, sm, then work seed stitch to second marker, sm, and continue working back sts as prev. Repeat seed stitch between 3rd and 4th markers. Seed st will be worked on all following rows on underarm sts only.

Waist shaping

Work body until 3" from underarm, then start decreasing as follows on next RS row: work to first marker, sm, p2tog, seed st to 2 sts before 2nd marker, k2tog, sm. 2 sts decr'd. Repeat on other side. Repeat decreases at 4.5" from underarm on next RS row: work to first marker, sm, k2tog, seed st to 2 sts before marker, p2tog, sm. Repeat at 6" as per first set of decreases.

AT THE SAME TIME, move the sts of Chart A on the back towards the center back by one st on the SAME ROWS you are decreasing as follows: after working first set of underarm seed sts, work to Chart A sts. M1L, work Chart A, then p2tog. Work to 2 sts before Chart A sts, p2tog, work Chart A sts, M1R. This will create a slight curve in the Chart A sts down the back.

Work until 7" from underarm, then start increasing by working to first marker, sm, M1L, seed st to 2nd marker, M1R, sm. 2 sts incr'd. Repeat on other side. Repeat increases at 8.5" and 10" from underarm. AT THE SAME TIME, move the sts of Chart A on the back away from the center back by one st on the SAME ROWS you are increasing as follows: After working first set of underarm seed sts, work to Chart A sts. P2tog, work Chart A, then M1L, work to Chart A sts, M1R, work Chart A sts, p2tog.

Work even until piece measures approx. 10 (10.5, 11, 11, 11.5, 12.25, 13)(13, 13, 13.25, 13.5, 13.75)" from underarm, ending on row 2, 4, 24, 26, 28 or 32 of Chart B. Change to smaller size 32" circ needles.

Next row (RS): Work all sts in seed st until you reach the first Chart B sts. K3, seed st 8 sts, K3. Seed st to underarm seed sts: If you have an even number of sts to work, start with a knit st, and if an odd number, start with a purl st. *Seed st to next Chart B sts, K3, seed st 8, K3, repeat from * two more times.
Next row (WS): *Work seed sts to Chart B sts, p3, seed st 8 sts, p3, repeat from * three more times.

Work as est. for 3 (3, 3, 3, 3, 3)(3.5, 3.5, 3.5, 3.5, 3.5)". BO all sts, in pattern, on a WS row.

Sleeves
Using larger size 16" circ needles, with RS facing and beg at center of underarm, pick up and knit 4 (4, 5, 5, 5, 5, 5)(5, 6, 6, 6, 7) sts. Then pick up and knit 22 (22, 21, 21, 22, 23, 23)(23, 22, 24, 24, 24) sts to start of saddle sts. Purl 5 (5, 5, 5, 5, 5, 5)(6, 6, 6, 6, 6), k13, p 5 (5, 5, 5, 5, 5, 5)(6, 6, 6, 6, 6) across saddle. Pick up and knit 22 (22, 21, 21, 22, 23, 23)(23, 22, 24, 24, 24) sts to start of underarm. Pick up and knit 4 (4, 5, 5, 5, 5, 5)(5, 6, 6, 6, 7) sts to center of underarm.

Pm and join for working in the round. 75 (75, 75, 75, 77, 79, 79)(81, 81, 85, 85, 87) sts total.

Shape Cap
The sleeve cap is worked back and forth in short rows whereby more sts are worked on each side of the saddle with each row. Work wraps together with their sts when you come to them. The cable from Chart B and purl sts on either side of it (as on the saddle) continue to be worked down the length of the sleeve until the cuff, while the remaining sts are knit.

Next rnd: With RS facing, work to end of saddle sts, wrap next st, turn work so WS is facing, work to other end of saddle sts, wrap next st and turn work.

Working the wraps tog with the wrapped sts when you come to them, work to 1 st past the turning gap, then wrap the next st on each side 7 (8, 5, 5, 5, 5, 5)(5, 4, 5, 5, 4) times.

Then work to the turning gap and work the next st after the gap

4 (2, 7, 7, 8, 9, 9)(9, 10, 10, 10, 12) times.

Then work 2 sts past the turning gap and wrap the next st at each side once.

Then work 3 (3, 4, 4, 4, 4, 4)(4, 5, 5, 5, 6) sts past the turning gap and wrap the next st each side once.

Work even in rounds for 1 (1, 1.5, 1.5, 1.5, 1.5, 1.5)(1.5, 1.5, 1.5, 1.5, 1.5)".

Shape Sleeve
Next rnd: K2tog, work to last 2 sts, ssk.

Repeat every 10th rnd 0 (0, 0, 0, 0, 0, 0)(6, 6, 4, 8, 3) times, then every 8th rnd 0 (0, 5, 7, 10, 9, 11)(4, 4, 7, 2, 8) times, then every 6th rnd 9 (9, 6, 4, 0, 2, 0)(0, 0, 0, 0, 0) times, then dec every 4th rnd 6 (5, 0, 0, 0, 0, 0)(0, 0, 0, 0, 0) times. Change to dpns when necessary.

43 (45, 51, 51, 55, 55, 55)(59, 59, 61, 63, 63) sts total.

Cont until sleeve measures 10.5 (11, 11.5, 12, 12.25, 12.5, 13)(13.25, 13.75, 14.25, 14.25, 14.25)" from underarm, ending on row 2, 4, 24, 26, 28 or 32 of Chart B. Change to smaller size dpns. Starting with a knit st, work all sts in seed st until the first st of Chart B. K3, seed st 8 sts, K3, then starting with a purl st, seed st to end of rnd. Continue to work as est for 5" or desired length, continuing decreases if necessary.

BO all sts in pattern.

Finishing
Buttonband
With smaller size 32" circ needles and RS facing, pick up and knit approx. 3 sts for every 4 rows along left front edge. Work in seed st for 3".

BO all sts on a WS row, in pattern.

Decide number and placement of buttons on buttonband and mark with removable markers on opposite front a few rows away from the edge.

Buttonhole Band
Work as for buttonband for 1.5", ending with a WS row. Work button holes opposite markers on next row as follows: With yarn in front, sl 1 st. Move yarn to back. *Sl 1 st, pass first sl st over second and off needle; repeat from * 3 more times. Sl last st on RH needle back to LH needle. Turn. Cable CO (see instructions) 4 sts, then CO 1 additional st, but before transferring new st to the LH needle, bring yarn to front between new st and first st on LH needle. Turn. Sl 1 st, pass first st over 2nd and off needle to close buttonhole. Repeat for each buttonhole as marked.

Work buttonhole band until it measures 3", then BO all sts on a WS row, in pattern.

Sew on buttons, weave in ends, and block to diagram.

Chart A

Chart B

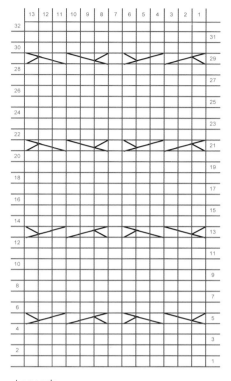

Legend:

knit
RS: knit stitch
WS: purl stitch

c3 over 3 left
RS: sl3 to CN, hold in front. k3, k3 from CN

c3 over 3 right
RS: sl3 to CN, hold in back. k3, then k3 from CN

K2tog, leaving sts on needle, then K first st again, sliping sts off needle

Skip next st, k following st through the back loop, leaving st on LH needle, then K slipped st through the front loop, slipping sts off needle

Note: when knitting in the rounf, read each row from right to left and work as a RS row. When knitting flat, read RS rows from right to left and WS rows from left to right.

Abbreviations

beg	Beginning
BO	Bind off (cast off)
circ	Circular
CO	Cast on
cont	Continue
dec	Decrease(s)
dec'd	Decreased
dpn(s)	Double pointed needle(s)
est	Established
inc	Increase
incr'd	Increased
k	Knit
k2tog	Knit 2 together (right slant-ing decrease)
LH	lLft hand
M1	Make 1 stitch: Insert left needle, from front to back, under strand of yarn which runs between next stitch on left needle and last stitch on right needle; knit this stitch through back loop. 1 stitch increased.
M1L	Make 1 Left: Insert left needle, from front to back, under strand of yarn which runs between next stitch on left needle and last stitch on right needle; knit this stitch through back loop. 1 stitch increased.
M1P	Make 1 Purl: Insert left needle, from front to back, under strand of yarn which runs between next stitch on left needle and last stitch on right needle; purl this stitch through back loop. 1 stitch increased.
M1R	Make 1 Right: Insert left needle, from back to front, under strand of yarn which runs between next stitch on left needle and last stitch on right needle; knit this stitch through front loop. 1 stitch increased.
p	Purl
pm	Place marker
prev	Previous
RH	Right hand
rnd	Round
RS	Right side
sl	Slip
sm	Slip marker
ssk	Slip 2 stitches individually as if to knit, then knit those 2 stitches together through the back loops (left-slanting decrease)
st(s)	Stitch(es)
tog	Together
WS	Wrong side

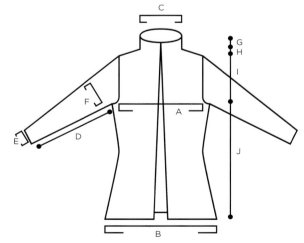

A 32 (34, 36, 38, 40, 42, 44)(46, 48, 50, 52, 54)"
B 32 (34, 36, 38, 40, 42, 44)(46, 48, 50, 52, 54)"
C 20 (20, 20, 20, 20, 20.5, 21.5)(23, 23.5, 23.5, 24, 24.5)"
D 15.5 (16, 16.5, 17, 17.25, 17.5, 18)(18.25, 18.75, 19.25, 19.25, 19.25)"
E 8.5 (9, 10.25, 10.25, 11, 11, 11,)(11.5, 11.5, 12, 12.5, 12.5)"
F 13.5 (13.5, 13.5, 14, 14.5, 14.5)(15, 15, 15.5, 15.5, 16)"
G 5"
H .75"
I 7.5 (7.5, 7.5, 7.75, 8, 8.25, 8.5)(8.5, 8.75, 9, 9.25, 9.5)"
J 13 (13.5, 14, 14, 14.5, 15.25, 16)(16.5, 16.5, 16.75, 17, 17.25)"

BAYR PULLOVER

by Jean Clement

FINISHED MEASUREMENTS

34.5 (40.5, 46, 51.5, 57.25)" finished chest measurement; garment is designed to fit a man's body and is meant to be worn with 2 to 4" of ease.

YARN

Knit Picks Wool of the Andes Worsted (100% Peruvian Highland Wool; 110 yards/50g):
Pampas Heather 24074 - 11 (12, 14, 16, 17) balls.

NEEDLES

US 7 (4.5mm) set of 4 dpns, 16 and 32" circular needles, or size to obtain gauge (larger sizes may choose to use a longer circular needle)

NOTIONS

Yarn Needle
Stitch Markers
Scrap yarn or stitch holder

GAUGE

24 sts and 26 rows = 4" in Twisted Stitch Yoke pattern, blocked.
20 sts and 25 rows = 4" in St st, blocked.

Bayr Pullover

Notes:

The nature of the differing gauges between the St st body and Twisted Stitch Yoke pattern naturally forms a slightly inset, square armhole. The sleeves are picked up around the armhole and worked to the cuff, incorporating the underarm sts similar to working a sock heel. The sleeves caps are worked in rows until all the underarm sts have been incorporated.

All references to Left and Right are as worn.

Cushy Rib Pattern (in the round over an even number of sts)
Round 1: *Sl 1, k1; rep from * to end of round.
Round 2: *K1, p1; rep from * to end of round.

Twisted Stitch Yoke Pattern (multiple of 14 sts + 3, worked flat)
Row 1 and 9 (WS): P1, k1, *p6, k1; rep from * to the last st, p1.
Row 2 (RS): K1, *p2, k3, T2R, k1, T2L, k3, p1; rep from * to the last 2 sts, p1, k1.
Row 3, 5, 7: P1, k1, *k1, p11, k2; rep from * to the last st, p1.
Row 4: K1, *p2, k2, T2R, k3, T2L, k2, p1; rep from * to the last 2 sts, p1, k1.
Row 6: K1, *p2, k1, T2R, k5, T2L, k1, p1; rep from * to the last 2 sts, p1, k1.
Row 8: K1, *p2, T2R, k7, T2L, p1; rep from * to the last 2 sts, p1, k1.
Row 10: K1, *k1, T2L, k3, p3, k3, T2R; rep from * to the last 2 sts, k2.
Row 11, 13, 15: P2, *p5, k3, p6; rep from * to the last st, p1.
Row 12: K1, *k2, T2L, k2, p3, k2, T2R, k1; rep from * to the last 2 sts, k2.
Row 14: K1, *k3, T2L, k1, p3, k1, T2R, k2; rep from * to the last 2 sts, k2.
Row 16: K1, *k4, T2L, p3, T2R, k3; rep from * to the last 2 sts, k2.

Rep Rows 1-16 for Twisted Stitch Yoke pattern.

Special Abbreviations

T2R – Twist 2 Right: K2tog, do not drop from needle, knit the first st again, drop both sts from needle.

T2L – Twist 2 Left: Slip 2 sts individually as if to knit, return to left needle retaining new orientation, knit the second st tbl, then knit both sts tog tbl, drop both sts from needle.

W&T – Wrap and Turn: Work to the stitch to be wrapped. On the knit side of work, bring yarn to the front of work, slip the next st as if to purl, take yarn to the back of work, turn work and slip the wrapped st to the RH needle. On the purl side of work, take yarn to the back of work, slip the next st as if to purl, bring yarn to the front of work, turn work and slip the wrapped st to the RH needle.

Picking Up Wraps/Closing the Gaps: Work to the wrapped st. On the knit side of work, insert tip of RH needle under the wrap and through the wrapped st knitwise. Knit the wrap together with the wrapped st. On the purl side of work, insert the tip of RH needle under wrap and lift it over the wrapped st onto the LH needle. Purl the wrap together with the wrapped st.

3-Needle Bind Off

Hold the two pieces of knitting together with the needle points facing to the right. Insert a third needle into the first stitch on each of the needles knitwise, starting with the front needle. Work a knit stitch, pulling the loop through both of the stitches you've inserted the third needle through. After you've pulled the loop through, slip the first stitch off of each of the needles. Repeat this motion, inserting your needle into one stitch on the front and back needles, knitting them together and slipping them off of the needles. Each time you complete a second stitch, pass the first finished stitch over the second and off of the needle (as you would in a traditional bind-off).

DIRECTIONS
Body

With longer circular needle loosely cast on 87 (101, 115, 129, 143) sts, pm, cast on 87 (101, 115, 129, 143) sts – 174 (202, 230, 258, 286) sts. PM and join to work in the round being careful to not twist sts.

Work Rounds 1-2 of the Cushy Rib Pattern for 2".

Change to St st and work even until body measures 16 (17.25, 17.5, 17.5, 17.5)" from cast on.

Place first 87 (101, 115, 129, 143) sts on waste yarn for front yoke.

Back Yoke

Work Rows 1-16 of the Twisted Stitch Yoke pattern until yoke measures 8 (8 1/2, 9, 9 1/2, 10)" from yoke division, ending after a WS row.

Shoulder Shaping

Row 1 (RS): Maintaining established pattern as much as possible, work 27 (31, 35, 41, 45) sts, W&T.
Row 2: Sl 1, work 12 (14, 16, 18, 20) sts, W&T.
Row 3: Sl 1, work to end, picking up wrap to close first short row gap, turn.
Row 4: Work 27 (31, 35, 41, 45) sts, W&T.
Row 5: Sl 1, work 12 (14, 16, 18, 20) sts, W&T.

Bayr Yoke Chart

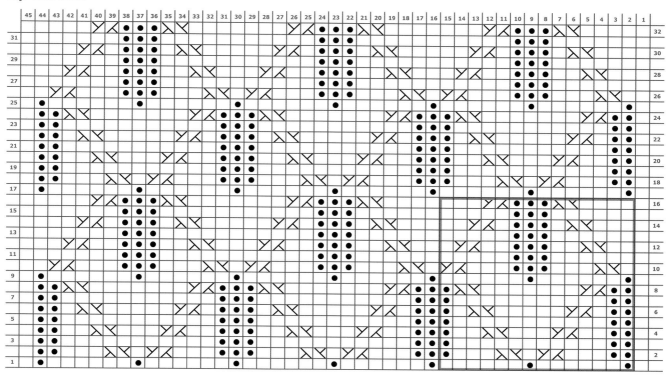

Legend:

knit
RS: knit stitch
WS: purl stitch

purl
RS: purl stitch
WS: knit stitch

Right Twist
Skip the first stitch, knit into 2nd stitch, then knit skipped stitch. Slip both stitches from needle together OR k2tog leaving sts on LH needle, then k first st again, sl both sts off needle.

Left Twist
sl1 to CN, hold in front. k1, k1 from CN

Row 6: Sl 1, work to end closing third short row gap, turn.
Row 7: Work across all sts, picking up wraps to close remaining short row gaps as you come to them.

Place all sts on scrap yarn.

Front Yoke

Place held yoke sts on longer circular needle and join yarn to begin a WS row.

Work Rows 1-16 of the Twisted Stitch Yoke pattern until yoke measures 6 1/2 (6 1/2, 7, 7, 7 1/2)" from division.

Divide for front neck

Neckline decreases and shoulder shaping happen at the same time, read through both sections before beginning.

Next Row: Continue in pattern as established over the first 35 (41, 46, 53, 58) sts, place center 17 (19, 23, 23, 27) sts on holder, join

new yarn and work remaining 35 (41, 46, 53, 58) sts in established pattern.

Working both sides of neck at the same time, and maintaining established pattern as much as possible, dec 1 st at each neck edge every RS row 8 (10, 10, 11, 12) times. Sizes 46, 51.5 and 57.25 only: At the same time, dec 1 st as est every WS row 1 (1, 1) times.

At the same time, when front yoke measures 8 1/2 (9, 9 1/2, 10, 10 1/2)" from division, begin shoulder shaping as follows, maintaining established pattern as much as possible:

Right Shoulder
Row 1 (WS): Work the first 14 (16, 18, 20, 22) sts, W&T.
Row 2: Sl 1, work to end of row.
Row 3: Work to end of row, closing short row gap.

Left Shoulder
Row 1 (WS): Work to the last 14 (16, 18, 20, 22) sts, W&T.

Row 2: Sl 1, work to end of row.

Row 3: Work to end of row, closing short row gap.

Place held stitches of Back on a needle. Matching 27 (31, 35, 41, 45) sts each of left and right shoulders with RS of front and back together, join one shoulder using 3-needle bind off, bind off center (33, 39, 45, 47, 53) back neck sts, join second shoulder using 3-needle bind off.

Sleeves

With RS facing and shorter circular needle, beginning at center of underarm pick up and knit 114 (120, 128, 132, 138) sts evenly spaced around armhole, place marker.

Row 1 (WS): Purl to 8 (9, 10, 11, 12) sts before marker, p2tog, turn.
Row 2: Sl 1, knit to 8 (9, 10, 11, 12) sts before marker, ssk, turn.

Rep Rows 1-2, slipping the first st of each row, and working to one fewer st before the marker than on the previous row, until all the underarm sts have been incorporated into the sleeve – 98 (102, 108, 110, 114) sts.

Continue in St st and begin working in the round. Work even for 9 (9, 9, 11, 10) rounds, then dec 1 st each side of marker every 2 rounds 32 (33, 35, 33, 35) times, changing to dpns when sts no longer fit comfortably around circular needle – 34 (36, 38, 44, 44) sts.

Work even until sleeve measures 16 (16 1/2, 17 1/2, 18, 18 1/2)" from underarm.

Work Rnds 1-2 of Cushy Rib Pattern for 2".

Loosely bind off all sts in pattern.

Collar

With RS facing and smaller circular needle, pick-up and knit 94 (106, 116, 126, 136) sts evenly spaced around neckline, pm and join to work in the round.

Work Rounds 1-2 of Cushy Rib pattern for 1 1/2".

Loosely bind off all sts in pattern.

Finishing

Weave in ends, wash and block to diagram.

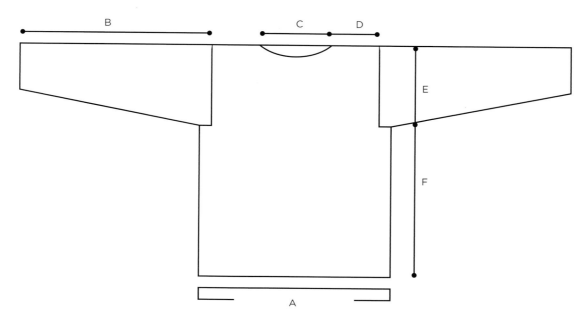

A 34.5 (40.5, 46, 51.5, 57.75)"
B 18 (18.5, 19.5, 20, 20.5)"
C 5.5 (6, 6, 6.5, 6.5)"
D 5.25 (5.5, 6, 6, 6.25)"
E 9 (9.5, 10, 10.5, 11)"
F 16 (17.25, 17.5, 17.5, 17.5)"

Abbreviations		PM	Place marker
BO	Bind off	rep	Repeat
CO	Cast on	RH	Right hand
dec	Decrease(s)	RS	Right side
DPN	Double pointed needles	SL	Slip
		St st	Stockinette stitch
est	Established	St(s)	Stitch(es)
K	knit	tbl	Through the back loop
K2tog	knit two sts together		
		WS	Wrong side
LH	Left hand	W&T	Wrap and Turn
P	Purl		

ARROWS HAT AND MITTS

by Stephannie Tallent

FINISHED MEASUREMENTS
Hat: 16.75 (19.25, 21.5, 24)" around brim.
8 (8.25, 8.5, 8.75)" tall.
Mitts: 8" palm circumference.
6" total length.

YARN
Knit Picks Wool of the Andes (100%
Peruvian Highland Wool; 110 yards/50g):
MC Haze Heather 26158, 2 (2, 3, 3) balls;
CC Blackberry 24273 1 ball.

NEEDLES
US 5 (3.75mm) DPNs or circular needles,
or one size smaller than size to obtain
gauge
US 6 (5mm) DPNs or circular needles, or
size to obtain gauge

NOTIONS
Yarn Needle
Stitch Markers (for Mitts: 3, one unique
for beginning of round; for Hat: 7 (8,
9, 10), one unique for beginning of
round; extra markers are used for noting
decrease sections)
Scrap yarn or spare needle for provisional
cast on

GAUGE
20 sts and 25 rows = 4" in stranded St st
in the round, blocked.
20 sts and 28 rows = 4" in St st in the
round, blocked.

Arrows Hat and Mitts

Notes:

This hat is worked from the brim up, with a provisional cast on and picot hem. If you prefer not to work a provisional cast on, simply fold and sew the picot hem.

The motif could easily be unisex. For a men's hat, work a plain hem (simply purl the turning row, rather than working (k2tog, yo), or work in (k2, p2) ribbing.

HAT DIRECTIONS
Brim

Using smallest needles and CC, provisionally CO 84 (96, 108, 120) sts. Join in the round, being careful not to twist. PM for beginning of round.

Knit 9 rounds.

Change to larger needles and MC.

Next round: (K2tog, yo) to end.

Knit 9 rounds.

Next round: Place provisionally cast on stitches onto a spare needle. Fold hem, WS together. Knit 2 sts tog, 1 from each needle.

Knit 3 rounds.

Arrow Repeat & Body of Hat

Next round: Begin working Round 1 of the Arrows chart, repeating chart 7 (8, 9, 10) times around.

Complete chart.

Knit until hat measures 4.75 (5, 5.5, 5.75)" from picot edge.

Crown decreases
Round 1: (K10, k2tog, pm) to last 12 sts, k10, k2tog.
Round 2: Knit.
Round 3: (Knit to 2 sts before marker, k2tog) around.
Round 4: Knit.

Rep Rounds 3 and 4 until you have 1 st between markers, ending on Round 3.

Last round: K2tog around, removing markers, finishing with k1 if you have an odd number of stitches.

Cut yarn, leaving a 10" tail. Thread yarn through live sts and pull snugly to close hole.

Finishing
Weave in ends, wash and block.

Optional Tassel:

Fold a 6" by 6" piece of cardboard in half. Place a 12" strand of yarn inside along the fold; you'll use this yarn to tie the top of the tassel. Wrap yarn (more for a thick tassel, less for a thinner tassel) around the cardboard. Pull the 12" strand of yarn against the tassel yarn at the open end of your cardboard. Cut the tassel yarn along the folded edge.

Tie the 12" strand at the top of the yarn. Cut 20" long strand. Wrap this strand around the tassel several times, about ½-3/4" from the top, and tie it snugly. Attach the tassel to the top of the hat. Make a second tassel if desired.

Arrows Hat Repeat

12	11	10	9	8	7	6	5	4	3	2	1	
		■				■				■		19
	■	■	■			■				■		18
■										■	■	17
■						■		■			■	16
		■						■				15
		■						■				14
			■					■				13
			■				■					12
							■					11
							■					10
												9
■		■						■		■		8
■		■						■		■		7
												6
		■						■				5
	■	■				■			■	■		4
	■	■				■		■	■	■		3
■	■									■		2
■		■				■				■		1

Legend:

☐ knit in MC

■ knit in CC

MITTS DIRECTIONS

Notes:

These mitts are worked with a provisional cast on and picot hem. If you prefer not to work a provisional cast on, simply fold and sew the picot hem.

The motif is graphic enough to be unisex. Feel free to swap out the picot hem for simple turned hems (just purl the turning round, rather than working (k2tog, yo)) or work (k1, p1) ribbing.

Bottom Cuff
Using smallest needles and CC, provisionally CO 42 sts. Join in the round, being careful not to twist. PM for beginning of round.

Knit 8 rounds.

Change to larger needles and MC.

Next round: (K2tog, yo) to end.

Knit 8 rounds.

Next round: Place provisionally cast on stitches onto a spare needle. Fold hem, WS together. Knit 2 sts tog, 1 from each needle.

Knit 1 round.

Main Body of Mitt

Right Mitt: K21, pm for gusset, k1, m1r, k1, pm for gusset, k19.

Left Mitt: K19, pm for gusset, k1, m1r, k1, pm for gusset, k21.

Next round: Begin working Left or Right Mitt chart.

Complete chart. Break CC yarn.

Knit 1 round.

Knit to gusset marker, place 19 sts between markers on waste yarn, remove gusset markers, CO 2 sts, knit to end.

Knit 4 rounds.

Switch to smaller needles. Work 6 rows garter stitch, beginning with a purl round. Bind off.

Thumb

Place sts back onto needles. Pick up 4 sts in the gap. 23 sts.

Knit 3 rounds. Switch to smaller needles.

Next round: (P2tog, p3) to 3 sts before end, p3. 19 sts.

Next 4 rounds: Work garter stitch, beginning with a knit round.

Bind off.

Finishing

Weave in ends, wash and block.

Legend:

- ☐ knit in MC
- ▨ knit in CC
- ▮ No Stitch
- ML make one right
- ML make one left

Left Mitt

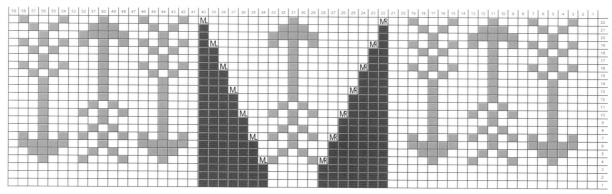

Right Mitt

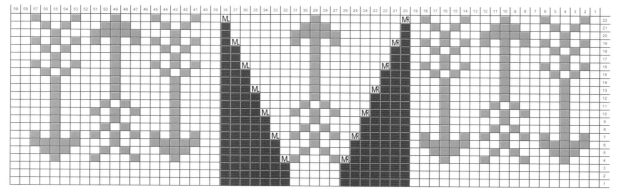

AMBERS PULLOVER & HAT

by Maureen Moody

FINISHED MEASUREMENTS

Pullover: 32 (33.5, 36.25, 39.25, 42.25, 46.5, 49.5, 51, 55.25, 58.25, 61)" finished bust measurement, worn with no ease.
Hat: Small 19", Large 20.5", with no ease.

YARN

Knit Picks Wool of the Andes Worsted (100% Peruvian Highland Wool; 110 yards/50g): A Merlot H. 25634, 9 (10, 11, 12, 13, 14, 15, 16, 17, 18, 20) balls; B Bittersweet H. 24652, 3 (3, 3, 3, 4, 4, 4, 4, 4, 4, 5) balls; C Persimmon H. 242801, (1, 1, 1, 1, 2, 2, 2, 2, 2, 2) balls; D Oyster H. 24949, 1 ball. Hat requires 1 additional ball of each color.

NEEDLES

US 7 (4.5mm) and US 6 (4.mm) 16" and 32" circular needles; DPNs or longer circular for Magic Loop technique or size to obtain stranded St st gauge
Needles 2 sizes smaller than St st gauge
Pullover option only: needles 3 sizes smaller for ribbing.

NOTIONS

Yarn needle
Stitch Markers
Scrap yarn or stitch holder
7" - 9" zipper
Sewing needle
Sewing thread matching Color B

GAUGE

22 sts and 25 rounds= 4" on US 7 needles in stranded St st in the round, blocked.
22 sts and 30 rounds = 4" on US 6 needles in St st in the round, blocked

Ambers Pullover & Hat

Notes:

Ambers is a circular yoke sweater, worked in the round from the top down, and featuring a stranded colorwork motif at yoke, hem and cuff. Stitches for yoke are increased in the Chart using the Backward Loop increase method, then Chart is continued over all stitches. For some sizes, the chart will continue into body and sleeve sections.

Pattern is written for both pullover and henley options, for either a woman or a man.

St st in the round

Knit every rnd.

Where a dash (-) is used instead of a number, that size does not take the indicated action.

Abbreviations

M1: (make one stitch) Insert left hand needle, from front to back, into the strand between right and left needles, then knit this strand through the back. 1 stitch increased.

K2tog: Knit two stitches together. 1 stitch decreased.

Ssk: Slip one stitch knitwise, then slip a second stitch knitwise. Insert left needle through the front of both stitches from left to right. Complete knit stitch by wrapping yarn around right needle and pulling through. 1 stitch decreased.

Techniques

German Twisted Cast On

The German Twisted method is very similar to the Long Tail cast on traditionally used. It creates a more flexible cast on with a distinctive edge.

Set-up: Begin as you would for the Long Tail method, with a long tail and a slip knot. Holding the needle in your righthand, hold both the tail and the yarn attached to the ball (working yarn) in the left hand. Slip your thumb and forefinger between the two strands, making sure the tail yarn is over your thumb. Open up your thumb and forefinger, creating a "V". The tail yarn is on your thumb, with the end attached to the needle crossing over the end held by the rest of your fingers. The working yarn is draped over your forefinger, with the end attached to the needle forming a "V" shape with the strand on your thumb.

Casting on:

1: Bring the needle toward you and under both strands on your thumb, then bring the needle down between the two strands on your thumb.

2: Wrap the yarn on your forefinger counter clockwise around the needle (in the same manner as making a knit stitch).

3: Bring the needle back down between the two strands on your thumb, then remove your thumb and cinch the stitch cast on. 1 stitch cast on.

Repeat for desired number of stitches.

Backward Loop

This method is used in cast on stitches and to work increases in the yoke.

Set-up: Hold yarn in your right hand. With your right thumb resting on top of the yarn, move your thumb down and toward you, wrapping the yarn around your thumb in the process. The end attached to the needle will be crossed under the end held in your hand.

1: Bring the needle up along your thumb and under the strand that is crossing under.

2: Remove your thumb and cinch the increased stitch. 1 stitch increased or cast on.

Repeat for desired number of stitches.

DIRECTIONS

Yoke

Pullover Option only:

Using smallest size [US 4 (3.5mm)]16" needle, Color B, and using the German Twisted cast on method, CO 72 (72, 72, 76, 76, 80, 84, 84, 92, 100, 104) sts. PM and join to work in the rnd at center back, careful not to twist.

Begin rib

All Rounds: *K2, p2; rep from * to end.

Work 1 more rnd in rib using Color B, then switch to Color A and cont in rib until measures 1" from CO edge.

Switch to stranded gauge16" needle.

Skip to "Both Options" below.

Henley Option only:

Using smallest size [US 4 (3.5mm)] 16" needle and Color B and using the German Twisted cast on, CO 72 (72, 72, 76, 76, 80, 84, 84, 92, 100, 104) sts. Do not join.

Begin Rib

Row 1: (RS) K3, *p2, k2; rep from * to last st, k1.
Row 2: (WS) P3, *k2, p2; rep from * to last st, p1.

Switch to Color A and cont in rib until measures 2.5" from CO edge, ending after a WS row.

Switch to stranded gauge [US 7 (4.5mm)]circular 16" needle.

Next row: (RS) Work in rib to end, PM, then using the Backward Loop method, CO 1 st, join to work in the rnd at center front.

Note: Henleyoption contains 1 extra st for the steek. This st is not included in future stitch counts. Work as follows:

With Color A, p1, work as specified for your size to end.

Continue in this manner until measures 7" for women's version or 9" for men's version from CO edge, then work the next rnd to last st, BO 3 sts for steek. Work next rnd to end.Using the Backward Loop method to CO 2 sts. Break yarn, leaving a tail to weave in.

In the next row after binding off and casting on at steek end, you must shift the beg of rnd from the center front to center back. Do so as follows:

If still working in the yoke, slip 144 (144, 156, 164, 176, 184, 196, 196, 212, 220, 232)sts, if working in the body, slip 88 (92, 100, 108, 116, 128, 136, 140, 152, 160, 168) sts, PM for new beg of rnd and work next rnd as specified for your size, rejoining body to work in the rnd when you reach the center front CO sts.

Both Options:
Size 32 and 33.5" only:
Skip to "Begin Chart A" below.

Sizes - (-, 36.25, 39.25, 43.75, 46.5, 49.5, 52.25, 55.25, 58.25, 62.5)":

Next rnd: Increase rnd K - (-, 3, 2, 2, 4, 7, 7, 4, 5, 4) sts, [k - (-, 11, 12, 6, 6, 5, 5, 6, 9, 8), M1] - (-, 6, 6, 12, 12, 14, 14, 14, 10, 12) times, k - (-, 3, 2, 2, 4, 7, 7, 4, 5, 4) sts to end.

72 (72, 78, 82, 88, 92, 98, 98, 106, 110, 116) sts on needle.

Begin Chart A
Work rnds 1-29 of Chart A, working increases using the Backward Loop method.

Change to stranded gauge 32" circular needlewhen there are too many sts to comfortably work on 16" needle.

When all increases are complete, 288 (288, 312, 328, 352, 368, 392, 392, 424, 440, 464) sts on needle.

Work 3 rows of stockinette st in color A

Begin Chart B
Work rnds 1-9 of Chart B.

Work 3 row stockinette st in color A.

Begin Chart C
Work rnds 1-7 of Chart C, Break Color B and work in Color A,switching to St st gauge [US 6 (4.mm)] 32" circular needle, and work in St st in the round.

AT THE SAME TIME
When yoke measures7.75 (8, 8.25, 8.75, 9.75, 10, 11, 11.75, 12, 12.25 12.5)" for women's, or [8.25, 8.75, 9.75, 10, 11, 11.75, 12.25, 12.5, 12.75, 13, 13.25)]" for men's from beginning of Chart A, skip to "Separate Body and Sleeves".

Note: For the Henleyoption, work steek BO as described above when measures 7" for a woman's version or 9" for a man fromCO edge.This may occur before or after Separate Body, and Sleeves, depending on size.

Separate Body and Sleeves
Next rnd: Work 42 (43, 46, 50, 53, 58, 61, 62, 67, 71, 74) sts (plus the steek st, if still working Henley Option), thread next 60 (58, 64, 64, 70, 68, 74, 72, 78, 78, 84) sts onto scrap yarn for sleeve, CO 4 (6, 8, 8, 10, 12, 14, 16, 18, 18, 20) sts for underarm, join to back and work 84 (86, 92, 100, 106, 116, 122, 124, 134, 142, 148), thread next 60 (58, 64, 64, 70, 68, 74, 72, 78, 78, 84) sts onto scrap yarn for sleeve, CO 4 (6, 8, 8, 10, 12, 14, 16, 18, 18, 20) sts for underarm, join to front and work final 42 (43, 46, 50, 53, 58, 61, 62, 67, 71, 74) sts. 176 (184, 200, 216, 232, 256, 272, 280, 304, 320, 336) sts rem for body.

Note: If still working in Chart B or C, make note of last chart row worked.

Body
If necessary, continue through Charts B and C, then switch to Color A,using St st gauge [US 6 (4.mm)] 32" needles;and work in St st in the round until measures 13.5 (13.5, 14, 14, 14.5, 14.5, 15, 15, 15, 15.5, 15.5,)"for a woman or 14.5 (14.5, 15, 15, 15.5, 15.5, 16, 16, 16.5, 16.5, 17)" for a man (or 2" less than desired length) from CO at underarm.

Begin Chart C
Switch to stranded gauge [US 7 (4.5mm)] needles.

Work Rnds 1-7 of Chart C.

K1 round plain.

Begin Rib
Switch to US 4 (3.5 mm),or smallest needle.

Next rnd: *K2, p2; rep from * to end.

Work in rib for 1", then switch to Color B and work 1 rnd in rib.

With Color B, BO all sts loosely in rib.

Sleeves
Place 60 (58, 64, 64, 70, 68, 74, 72, 78, 78, 84) sleeves sts on same size needles being used at Separate Body and Sleeves row,DPNs, two 24" needles, or one 32" needle.

With RS facing, join Color A and pick up and knit 4 (6, 8, 8, 10, 12, 14, 16, 18, 18, 20) sts in CO at underarm, PM for beg of rnd at the center of these sts. 64 (64, 72, 72, 80, 80, 88, 88, 96, 96, 104) sts on needle.

If necessary, continue through Charts B and C, then switch to Color A, using St st gauge [US 6 (4.mm)] DPNs or two 24" circular needles for two circular technique or one 32" or longer circular for Magic Loop technique, and work in Stst in the round until sleeve measures 4" for a woman or 5" for a man from CO at underarm.

Begin Sleeve Shaping
Next rnd: Decrease Rnd K1, k2tog, knit to last 3 sts, ssk, k1. 2 sts decreased.

62 (62, 70, 70, 78, 78, 86, 86, 94, 94, 102) sts rem on needle.

Rep Decrease Rnd every 5 (5, 5, 5, 5, 5, 5, 5, 4, 5, 4)th rnd 11 (11, 11, 11, 11, 11, 11, 11, 15, 11, 15) more times.

40 (40, 48, 48, 56, 56, 64, 64, 64, 72, 72) sts rem on needle.

Work even in St st in the round until sleeve measures 13.5 (14, 14, 14.5, 14.5, 14.5, 15, 15, 15.5, 15.5, 15.5)" for a woman or 15 (15, 15, 15.5, 16.5, 17, 17, 17.5, 17.5, 18, 18)" for a man (or 3" less than desired sleeve length), from picked up stsat underarm.

Begin Chart C
Using stranded gauge [US 7 (4.5mm)] needles, work Rnds 1-7 of Chart C.

K1 round plain.

Begin Rib
Using smallest [US 4 (3.5mm)] 32"needle.

Next rnd: *K2, p2; rep from * to end.

Work in rib for 2", then switch to Color B and work 1 rnd in rib.

With Color B, BO all sts loosely in rib.

Rep for second sleeve.

Finishing

Weave in ends. Wash and block to diagram.

Henley Option only:

After blocking, prepareand cut steek along front center purl st.

For information on preparing and cutting a steek, view our tutorial: http://www.knitpicks.com/wptutorials/steeking/

With RS facing, using smallest[US 4 (3.5mm)] 32" circular needle and Color B, pick up and knit 2 sts for every 3 rows down left front steek edge, pick up and knit 2 sts in sts CO at center front, then pick up and knit 2 sts for every 3 rows up right front steek edge.

Knit 4 rows, then BO all sts loosely as knit sts.

Sew in zipper.

For information on installing a zipper, view our tutorial: www.knitpicks.com/wptutorials/Zippers

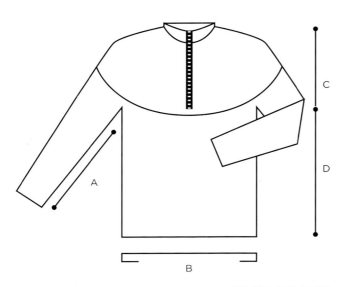

A   W 18 (18, 18.25, 18.25, 18.5, 18.5, 18.75, 18.75, 18.5, 18.5, 18.5)"
    M 19 (19, 19.5, 19.5, 20, 20, 19.75, 19.75, 19.5, 19.5, 19.5)"

B   32 (33.5, 36.25, 39.25, 42.25, 46.5, 49.5, 51, 55.25, 58.5, 61)"

C   W 7.75 (8, 8.25, 8.75, 9.75, 10, 11, 11.75, 12, 12.25, 12.5)"
    M 8.25 (8.75, 9.75, 10, 11, 11.75, 12.25, 12.5, 12.75, 13, 13.25)"

D   W 15.5 (15.5, 16, 16, 16.5, 16.5, 17, 17, 17, 17.5, 17.5)"
    M 16.5 (16.5, 17, 17, 17.5, 17.5, 18, 18, 18.5, 18.5, 19)"

Chart A

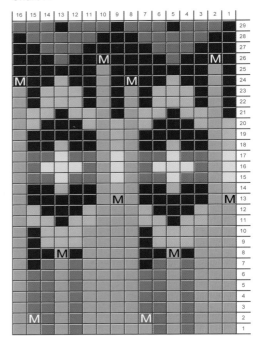

Chart B

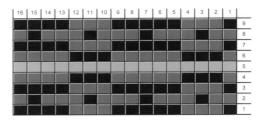

Chart C

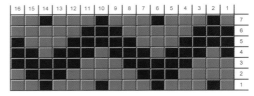

Legend:

No Stitch

knit
knit stitch

make one

M   Make one by lifting strand in between stitch just worked and the next stitch, knit into back of this thread.

A Merlot H

B Bittersweet H

C Persimmon H

D Oyster H

Ambers Hat

Notes:

Ambers Hat is worked in the round from the top down, using Magic loop. Round 8 is for smaller size hat.

DIRECTIONS

With larger needle using color A, CO 6,[7] sts. Using magic loop Place 3,[4] sts on one needle 3 sts on other needle. Join in the round careful not to twist. Place marker.

Round 1 - K

Round 2 - K1, M1 repeat till end. (12,[14] sts)

Round 3 - K

Round 4 - K1,(m1, K2) repeat till last st,k(18, [21]sts)

Round 5 - K

Round 6 - K1, (m1, K3) repeat till last 2 sts k2 (24,[28] sts)

Round 7 - K

This round is only for smaller size hat

Round 8 - K1, m1, k12, m1, k11. (26 sts)

Work the pattern chart working all M1 increases as backward loops increases. Work till row 42 (104sts,[112sts]). Switch to smaller needles for ribbing then complete Round 4243-48. (104, 112 sts sts.)

Bind Off Loosely.

Finishing

Weave in ends, wash and block.

Abbreviations		rem	remain(ing)
BO	Bind off	rep	Repeat
CO	Cast on	Rnd	Round
cont	Continue	RS	right side
DPN	Double pointed	SM	Slip marker
	needles	SSK	sl, sl, k these 2 sts
K	Knit		together
K2tog	Knit two sts to-gether	St(s)	Stitch(es)
		St st	Stockinette stitch
M1	Make 1 stitch	WS	Wrong side
PM	Place marker		

REILLY AFGHAN

by Kerin Dimeler-Laurence

FINISHED MEASUREMENTS
40x64"

YARN
Knit Picks Wool of the Andes (100% Peruvian Highland Wool; 110 yards/50g): Larch Heather 25989, 30 balls.

NEEDLES
US 8 (5mm) long circular needles, or size to obtain gauge
Long circular needles one size smaller than those used to obtain gauge

NOTIONS
Tapestry Needle
Yarn Needle
Stitch Markers
Cable Needle

GAUGE
26 sts and 32 rows = 4" in Cable pattern, blocked.

Reilly Afghan

Notes:

Seed Stitch, worked over an even number of sts:

Row 1: (K1, P1) across row.

Row 2: (P1, K1) across row.

DIRECTIONS

A border of seed stitch surrounds a large cable panel.

With smaller needles, CO 206 sts. Work in Seed st for 16 rows; on the last row, place markers after the first 16 and before the last 16 sts.

Charts

On the next row, switch to larger needles and begin working from Right, Center and Left charts between markers, following Chart Reading Instructions. While working the charts in the center, maintain the Seed st pattern on the outer 16 sts.

After working the last row of the charts, 206 sts remain on the needles. Switch to smaller needles and work in Seed st for 16 rows.

BO all sts.

Finishing

Weave in ends. Wash and block to measurements.

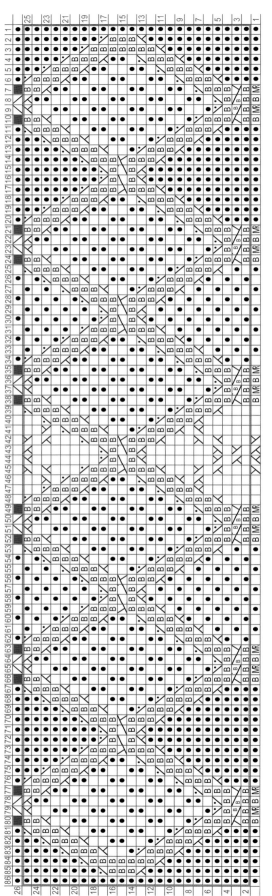

Center Chart

Legend:

⊙ **purl**
RS: purl stitch
WS: knit stitch

MR **make one right**
PU the bar between st just worked and next st and place on LH needle backwards (incorrect stitch mount). Knit through the front of the loop.

☐ **knit**
RS: knit stitch
WS: purl stitch

M **make one left**
PU the bar between st just worked and next st and place on LH needle mounted as a regular knit stitch; knit through the back of the loop.

■ **No Stitch**
Placeholder - No stitch made.

B **knit tbl**
RS: Knit stitch through back loop
WS: Purl stitch through back loop

c2 over 1 left P
RS: sl2 to CN, hold in front. p1, k2 from CN

◇ **bobble**
To make bobble: (k1 yo k1 yo k1) in one stitch, turn and p5. Turn and k5. Turn and p2tog, p1, p2tog. Turn and sl1-k2tog-psso, completing bobble

c2 over 1 right P
sl1 to CN, hold in back. k2, p1 from CN

c2 over 2 left
sl 2 to CN, hold in front. k2, k2 from CN

c2 over 2 right
sl2 to CN, hold in back. k2, k2 from CN

≥ **Make 1 Purlwise**
Perform a lifted bar increase, purling into the new st.

Left Twist
sl1 to CN, hold in front. k1, k1 from CN

Right Twist
Skip the first stitch, knit into 2nd stitch, then knit skipped stitch. Slip both stitches from needle together OR k2tog leaving sts on LH needle, then k first st again, sl both sts off needle.

c2 over 2 left P
sl 2 to CN, hold in front. p2, k2 from CN

c2 over 2 right P
sl2 to CN, hold in back. k2, p2 from CN

k2tog
WS: Purl 2 stitches together

ssk
WS: Purl two stitches together in back loops, inserting needle from the left, behind and into the backs of the 2nd & 1st stitches in that order

c2 TBL over 1 left P
sl2 to CN, hold in front. p1, k2 TBL from CN

c2 TBL over 1 right P
sl1 to CN, hold in back. k2 TBL, p1 from CN

c2 TBL over 2 left
sl 2 to CN, hold in front. k2 TBL, k2 TBL from CN

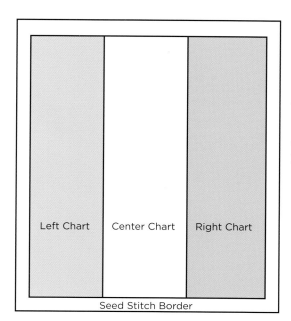

Seed Stitch Border

Chart Instructions
Charts are worked flat; read RS rows (odd numbers) from right to left and WS rows (even numbers) from left to right. On RS rows, work across Right Chart, then Center Chart, then Left Chart; on WS rows, work across Left Chart, then Center Chart, then Right Chart.

Work across RS row 1 of Right, Center, and Left charts; 50 sts added on row 1. 256 sts.

Begin working repeats of all charts: Work rows 2-49 of Right and Left charts 10 times; work rows 2-25 of Center Chart 20 times. After all repeats are worked, move on to the last row of each chart; 50 sts decreased on final row. 206 sts.

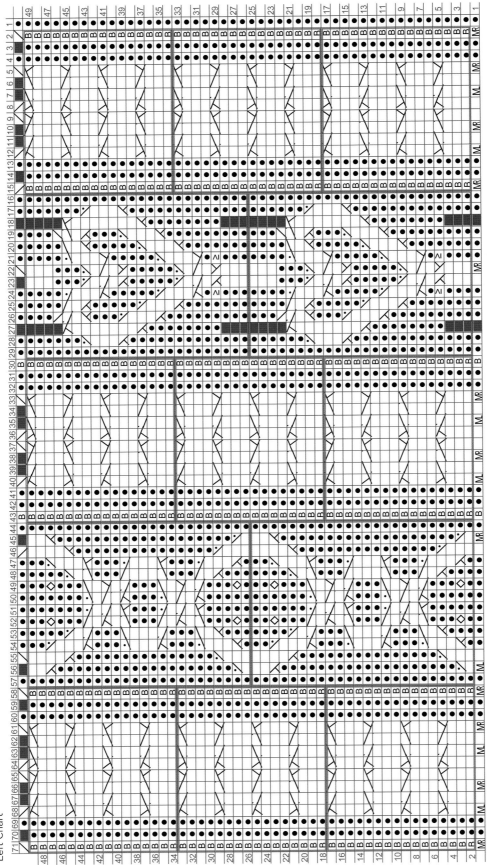

Left Chart

Right Chart

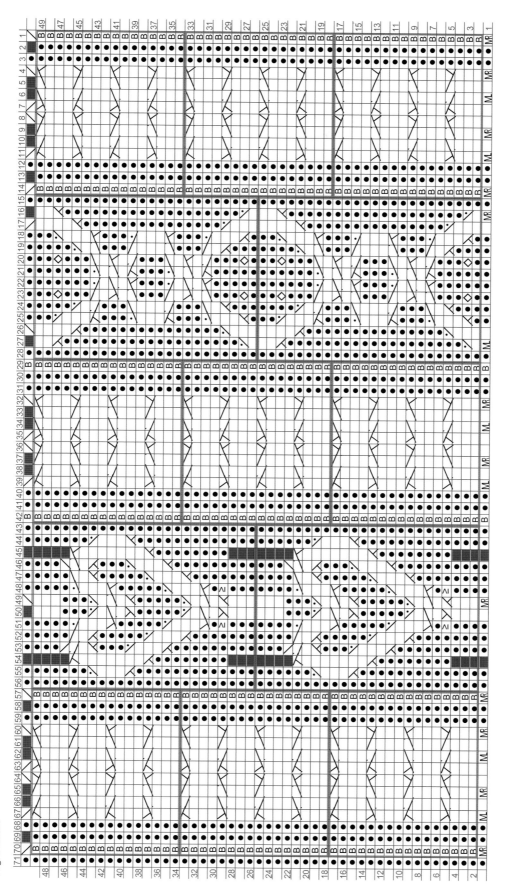

Knit Picks yarn is both luxe and affordable—a seeming contradiction trounced! But it's not just about the pretty colors; we also care deeply about fiber quality and fair labor practices, leaving you with a gorgeously reliable product you'll turn to time and time again.

This collection features

Wool of the Andes
Worsted Weight

100% Peruvian Highland Wool

Wool of the Andes Tweed
Worsted Weight

80% Peruvian Highland Wool, 20% Donegal Tweed

View this beautiful yarn and more at www.KnitPicks.com